WARBIRDS ILLUSTRATED No 39

AF574765

1. A pair of RF-4C Phantoms from the Idaho Air National Guard's 190th Tactical Reconnaissance Squadron taking off from Andrews AFB for a photo-recce sortie during the 'Photo Derby' competition, April 1982. The Air Guard provides seven photo-recce squadrons to augment Tactical Air Command's recce force. (Don Linn)

WARBIRDS ILLUSTRATED No 39

Tactical Air Command

DON LINN & DON SPERING

a&ap

ARMS AND ARMOUR PRESS

Introduction

Published in 1986 by Arms & Armour Press Ltd., 2–6 Hampstead High Street, London NW3 1QQ.

Distributed in the United States by Sterling Publishing Co. Inc., 2 Park Avenue, New York, N.Y.10016.

British Library Cataloguing in Publication Data:
Linn, Don
Tactical air command.
1. United States. *Air Force* – Pictorial works
2. Airplanes, Military – United States – Pictorial works
I. Title II. Spering, Don
623.74′6′0973 UG1243

ISBN 0-85368-752-8

Editing, design and artwork by Roger Chesneau.
Typesetting by Typesetters (Birmingham) Ltd.
Printed and bound in Italy
by GEA/GEP in association with
Keats European Ltd., London.

◀2

2. An A-7D Corsair II plugs into a KC-135 tanker following a practice bombing sortie. The A-7D is classified as a subsonic close air support aircraft with limited interdiction capabilities. A total of 459 single seat A-7D Corsairs were delivered to the USAF between 1968 and 1976, 383 of these later being modified to carry the Pave Penny laser target designator pod. (Don Linn)

Tactical Air Command is one of the major commands making up the organizational structure of the US Air Force. It is responsible for all tactical air operations in the continental United States, and for the air defence of North America.

TAC was established on 21 March 1946, a year before the Air Force became a separate service from the US Army, and during the past forty years it has experienced many changes, the most prominent of these being the transfer of all tactical airlift assets to the Military Airlift Command (MAC) in 1974 and the incorporation of all Aerospace Defense Command assets into TAC in 1979 (the latter move bringing about the new designation Air Defense TAC, more commonly referred to as ADTAC).

Tactical Air Command organizational structure includes ADTAC as a sub-command and two numbered air forces, the 9th and the 12th; it also includes three weapons centres, an airborne warning and control division, and a separate division in Panama. But the greatest augmenting forces are the Air National Guard, which has eighteen wings with combat-ready crews, and the Air Force Reserve, whose assets represent a considerable percentage of TAC's fighter strength.

During the past forty years TAC has responded to many crises throughout the world, sending its mobile forces to serve during the Korean War, the Berlin Airlift, the Cuban Missile Crisis and the Vietnam conflict in order to counter threats to US interests and world peace. TAC's greatest contribution by far was during the Vietnam War, when its fighter, reconnaissance, special operations, electronic warfare and airlift units took part in all areas of combat operations.

TAC was again called upon during the October 1973 Middle East Crisis to counter the Soviet threat to the balance of power in that unstable region. TAC sent a squadron of F-4C Phantoms on an eleven-hour, non-stop flight from the United States to Israel, C-130s following less than three days later with equipment and support personnel. In March 1979 TAC again responded to trouble in that region, deploying its E-3A AWACS aircraft at the request of the Saudi government to monitor the border clashes between North and South Yemen. These deployments demonstrate the Command's ability to react quickly with a variety of military aircraft and support personnel to any threat.

For the future, few changes in organization are expected, but new machines like the McDonnell Douglas F-15E, the General Dynamics F-16XL and the Advanced Tactical Fighter (ATF) will form the backbone of its fighter forces to the year 2000 and beyond. The Air Force Reserve and Air National Guard will continue to play major roles in TAC and will have the benefit of receiving more modern aircraft better to fulfil their responsibilities. Indeed, TAC's second forty years will be an exciting as well as a challenging time.

Don Linn and Don Spering

▲3 ▼4

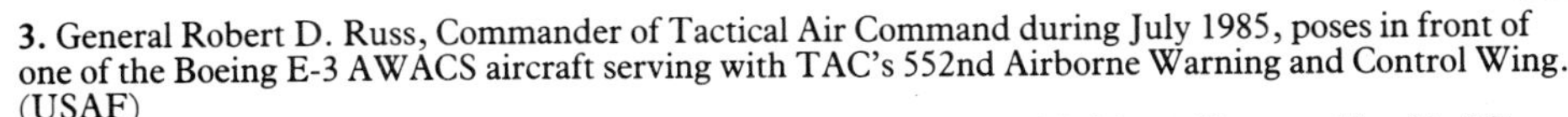

5▲

3. General Robert D. Russ, Commander of Tactical Air Command during July 1985, poses in front of one of the Boeing E-3 AWACS aircraft serving with TAC's 552nd Airborne Warning and Control Wing. (USAF)
4. Prior to the 1970s TAC aircraft were maintained in a natural metal finish, as illustrated by this RF-84F of the Alabama Air National Guard photographed in 1963. Characteristic of this early scheme is the lightning bolt through the TAC badge on the Thunderflash's tail. (P. Stevens/Don Spering)
5. Serving as front-line fighters with Tactical Air Command during the 1950s and early 1960s until replaced by late model F-100D Super Sabres, Republic F-84Fs continued in use with Air National Guard squadrons for some time afterwards. This Thunderstreak was assigned to Illinois' 169th Tactical Fighter Squadron, one of the last veterans of the early jet era and finally replaced in the Air Guard by F-4C Phantoms. (P. Stevens/Don Spering)
6. During the height of its service in 1955, the F-84F equipped twelve fighter wings, six of which were assigned to SAC. This version of the F-84, an attempt by Republic to extend the life of its earlier straight-winged F-84E, made its maiden flight under the designation YF-96A and a total of 2,711 Thunderstreaks were produced. (Don Spering)

6▼

▲7

▲8 ▼9

7. A photo-reconnaissance RF-84 Thunderflash with two 450-gallon fuel tanks, on final approach to Shaw AFB following an August 1970 training mission. The two external fuel tanks gave the F-84 and RF-84 a range of 1,240 miles, whilst in-flight refuelling gave the aircraft a range that was limited only by the pilot's endurance and the aircraft's mechanical condition. (Jim Sullivan)

8. As with the F-84F Thunderstreak, the RF-84 Thunderflash found new life and extended service with Air National Guard squadrons. A total of 715 RF-84s were produced by Republic to meet the USAF's requirements for a replacement for Lockheed's RF-80. The prototype YRF-84F, serial 51-1828, was completed in February 1952, and production aircraft equipped USAF, and later Air National Guard, squadrons into the early 1970s until replaced by RF-101 Voodoos. This RF-84 was assigned to the 171st TRS, Michigan ANG. (F. Roos)

9. At first glance this F-86H appears similar to the standard F-86 Sabre, but closer examination shows that four guns instead of six are carried in the nose and that the fuselage is deeper and longer. The first flight of the F-86H took place on 27 October 1953, but accidents, including one that claimed the life of the famous test pilot and Korean War ace Capt. Charles McConnell, delayed its procurement by the USAF. Pictured here is an F-86H of the 138th Tactical Fighter Squadron ('The Boys from Syracuse'). (Jim Sullivan)

10. Although the F-86H experienced delays in entering USAF service and never really met all USAF requirements, this last version of the Sabre jet saw US military duty from 1955 until the very early 1970s. The F-86H illustrated here served with the 175th TFG of the Maryland Air Guard until 1972, when the unit re-equipped with the Cessna A-37. (Don Spering)

11. An RF-101C of the 29th Tactical Reconnaissance Squadron based at Shaw AFB during the 1970s. A derivative of the original F-101, this photo-reconnaissance version of the Voodoo bore the brunt of such duties during the Vietnam War until the mid-1960s, when it was replaced by the RF-4 Phantom. In its day, of course, the RF-101 had replaced the RF-84. (Don Spering)

12. An RF-101A Voodoo belonging to the 31st Tactical Reconnaissance Squadron, returns from an April 1970 training mission. In 1954 Tactical Air Command ordered two prototype YRF-101A Voodoos, the first of which made its first flight in May 1956; a year later production RF-101As were being delivered to the 63rd TRW, whilst the first of 166 RF-101Cs flew in July 1958. (Jim Sullivan)

10▲

11▲ 12▼

▲13

13. An EB-66C of the 19th Tactical Electronics Reconnaissance Squadron lands at Itazuke Air Base, Japan, following the completion of a March 1969 training sortie. The EB-66 was modified from the B-66 originally manufactured from 1954 to 1959 and scheduled to be retired in the 1960s, but the Vietnam War found new service for this old warhorse. (Jim Sullivan/Don Spering)

14. A Helio U-10B Courier of the 5th Air Commando Squadron. The U-10 possessed excellent STOL capabilities, making it a valuable asset for behind-the-lines missions in Vietnam, often supplying isolated US Army Special Forces camps. (Don Spering)

▼14

15▲

15. During the early 1970s, with the winding down of US involvement in the Vietnam War, many types such as the U-10 Courier were no longer needed by the Air Force, their specialized missions requiring only a limited number of aircraft assigned to TAC. The Courier, however, was able to find new duties serving with some of the Air National Guard units, such as Rhode Island's 143rd Special Operations Squadron in 1973. (Don Spering)

16. Throughout its service career, from 1956 to the early 1970s, the F-102 was not known as a TAC fighter, instead finding duty with Fighter Interceptor Squadrons assigned to Air Defense Command. However, a few PQM-102 piloted drones flew with TAC's 82nd Tactical Air Target Squadron at Tyndall AFB during the 1982 'William Tell' competition. (Don Spering)

16▼

▲17 ▼18

19▲

17. By the time this photograph was taken in 1984 the F-100D Super Sabre had long since been withdrawn from front-line service with TAC, yet several are still operated as piloted YQF-100D drones by the 82nd Tactical Air Target Squadron at Tyndall AFB, Florida, as participants in the 'William Tell' competitions. (Don Spering)
18. After retirement from front-line TAC squadrons, F-100C/Ds were handed down to the Air National Guard and the Air Force Reserve, giving the Super Sabre an effective service life into the mid-1970s. Illustrated here is an F-100C of the 110th Tactical Fighter Squadron of the Missouri ANG based at St. Louis, 20 May 1970. (F. Roos)
19. This 1969 photograph of an F-100D of the 524th TFS, taken shortly before the unit's conversion to F-111s at Cannon AFB, New Mexico, illustrates the Vietnam-era camouflage applied to TAC fighters as a result of that conflict. The natural metal finish common to USAF machines from the late 1940s through to the early 1960s was found to be impractical for combat service. (Don Spering)
20. The flight-line of the 69th Tactical Fighter Training Squadron at Luke AFB, Arizona, in 1974, featuring a row of TF-104Gs. In 1955 Lockheed received an order for 155 F-104As, all for Air Defense Command; the first F-104C Starfighter for TAC appeared in 1958. During the Vietnam War F-104Cs were first deployed to counter the MiG threat, but they finished their combat service as air-to-ground fighter bombers. (Don Spering)

20▼

21. A Republic F-105B Thunderchief, refuelling probe extended, about to hook up to an Air Force KC-135 tanker following a gunnery training sortie in 1978. This version of the Thunderchief was limited to drogue-and-probe refuelling, but the F-105D could also refuel from a straight tanker boom, by means of a nose-mounted receptacle directly in front of the windscreen. (Don Linn)

22. The 508th Tactical Fighter Squadron of the Air Force Reserve at Hill AFB was also a recipient of the F-105B when TAC re-equipped with F-105Ds. The first flight of the F-105B took place in 1958, and a total of 833 Thunderchiefs were produced by Republic in three basic versions – the F-105B, -D and -F. Thirty F-105Ds were converted to 'T-Stick II' improved all-weather bomber variants, and the F-105F two-seat trainer was later modified to become the F-105G Wild Weasel for SAM missile suppression duties in Vietnam. (Don Spering)

23. A pair of F-105Ds of the District of Columbia (Washington, DC) Air Guard take off from their home base at Andrews AFB for a 1978 practice bombing sortie. In 1957 the Air Force requested Republic to convert the F-105B to an all-weather strike fighter, and the resulting F-105D prototype made its first flight on 9 June 1959. (Don Linn)

24. An F-105D 'T-Stick II' of the Air Force Reserve's 457th Tactical Fighter Squadron (based at Carswell AFB) photographed over the Texas desert during a February 1982 training flight. Thirty F-105Ds were retrofitted with the Thunderstreak II fire control system – easily identified by the enlarged spine on this F-105 – and thereby increased the aircraft's all-weather bombing accuracy seven-fold. (Don Spering)

◀**21**

22▲

23▲ 24▼

▲25

25. A trio of two-seat Thunderchiefs belonging to the Georgia ANG's 128th Tactical Fighter Squadron: the two Thunderchiefs with the 'sharkmouth' nose are F-105G Wild Weasels, the third aircraft an F-105F trainer. Externally both types look the same, but a close examination reveals that the F-105Gs are fitted with ECM equipment along the fuselage, beneath the wing root. During the Vietnam War these Wild Weasel Thunderchiefs proved very effective in dealing with the surface-to-air missile threat over North Vietnam. (Don Spering)

26. 'High Time Thud' painted on the nose of this F-105D, serial 62-347, of the Air Force Reserve's 466th Tactical Fighter Squadron based at Hill AFB, is a reference to 6,700-plus flying hours accumulated, the highest number for any F-105 and a total achieved during June 1983 while the aircraft was on a training sortie. Eight months later, during February 1984, the Thunderchief was retired from service during ceremonies at Hill AFB. (Don Spering)

▼26

27▲

27. The last ANG Thunderchief, F-105F serial 63-8299, of Georgia Air Guard's 128th Tactical Fighter Squadron, on its last flight, accompanied by its F-4D successor. Nearly a dozen F-105s were flown to Patuxent River to be prepared as targets for the nearby US Army Aberdeen Proving Grounds – a rather unglamorous end to such an outstanding fighter. (Don Spering)

28. An A-7D of the 357th Tactical Fighter Squadron, 355th Tactical Fighter Wing, based at Davis-Monthan AFB, Arizona and photographed here on 10 February 1972. The Air Force A-7D, derived from the Navy's A-7 series, first began its TAC duties in 1968, and a total of 459 aircraft were delivered to Air Force and TAC squadrons. By 1980, however, most A-7Ds were serving with Air Guard squadrons. (N. Taylor)

28▼

▲29

29. One of the thirteen A-7D Air Guard squadrons is the 124th TFS, one of whose machines is seen here flying off the wing of a KC-135 tanker during a July 1982 refuelling rendezvous. (Don Spering)

30. Six A-7Ds from the 120th Tactical Fighter Squadron, Colorado Air Guard, stack up below a KC-135 tanker for this 24 February 1984 photograph. Of interest here is the contrast between the new 'European 1' camouflage scheme applied to four of the Corsairs and the previous Vietnam-style finish. There also appears to be considerable weathering on the upper wing surfaces of the lead aircraft. (Don Spering)

▼30

31▲

31. An A-7D Corsair from the Colorado Air Guard's 120th Tactical Fighter Squadron photographed from the boom operator's position in the belly of a KC-135 tanker. The snow-covered Colorado countryside below is in marked contrast to the 'European I' camouflage applied to this A-7, which appears to lack national insignia. The black stripe on the leading edge of the tail is a VHF/LORAN antenna. (Don Spering)

32. A Virginia Air Guard A-7D on its way to the bombing range in 1984. Barely visible on the outboard pylon-mounted MER are blue, sand-filled BDU-33 practice bombs. The A-7 will make a conventional bomb run and release the practice bomb, and upon impact a smoke charge is set off to help range personnel evaluate the hits. (Don Spering)

32▼

▲33

33. A two-seat A-7K serving with the 149th Tactical Fighter Squadron of the Virginia Air Guard on final approach during the summer of 1985. This A-7K, appearing in 'European I' camouflage, has very subdued serial numbers and national insignia. Attached to the outboard pylon is a travel pod used by aircrews to carry personal belongings during extended deployments. (Don Linn)

34. On 1 July 1983 the 157th Tactical Fighter Squadron of the South Carolina Air Guard became the first ANG unit to re-equip with F-16 Fighting Falcons. The F-16 is bringing an important improvement in capability to the Air Guard, and more F-16 squadrons will follow. (Don Spering)

35. An A-37B assigned to Maryland Air Guard's 104th Tactical Fighter Squadron seen during a 1977 training flight. Developed from the Cessna T-37 trainer for FAC (Forward Air Control) duties in Vietnam, the A-37 currently equips only one TAC squadron outside the Air Guard and Reserves – the 602nd Tactical Air Control Wing at Davis-Monthan AFB. However, non-TAC A-37s have recently been assigned to the 511th Tactical Control Group based at Osan Air Base, Korea. (Don Spering)

36. An OA-37B of the 182nd Tactical Air Support Group, Illinois Air Guard, on a 1982 FAC training sortie. The OA-37 and A-37B are almost identical, the only difference being the former's new radios (the antennas for which can be seen attached to the leading edge of the horizontal stabilizers and positioned behind the cockpit). The nose-mounted refuelling probe, along with the two wingtip tanks and four underwing pylon-mounted tanks, give the Cessna considerable range. (Don Spering)

37. A Pennsylvania Air Guard A-37B, off the wing of his flight leader, having just completed an FAC training sortie, autumn 1982. Twenty-five A-37s were sent to Vietnam for a year-long evaluation in which not one was lost to enemy fire although more than 10,000 combat sorties were flown. Nearly 400 A-37s were produced by Cessna, many being delivered to the South Vietnamese Air Force and eventually lost. (Don Spering)

▼34

35▲

36▲ 37▼

▲38 ▼39

40▲

38. Sitting on the ramp in front of Hangar 2 at MacDill AFB in 1972 is perhaps the end of the USAF Phantom pedigree – an F-4E of the 1st Tactical Fighter Wing. The F-4E was developed as an improved version of the F-4D, the principal change being the addition of an M-61A1 Vulcan cannon under the nose. The first production F-4E was delivered to TAC in 1967. (Don Spering)

39. An F-4D Phantom of the 56th TFTW – one of the TAC training wings where new F-4 pilots were taught their craft – at MacDill AFB in 1979. The F-4D was developed from the F-4C and included several major design changes to incorporate the APQ-109 fire-control radar, ASN-63 inertial navigation system and various computer upgrades. The first flight for the F-4D took place on 8 December 1968; a total of 843 aircraft were produced, 32 of which were supplied to Iran and eighteen to Korea. (Don Linn)

40. An F-4C of the 110th Tactical Fighter Squadron, Missouri Air Guard, during a 1982 flight. The introduction of F-4Ds and F-4Es to TAC in 1966 and 1967 respectively meant that the F-4C was becoming outdated, and the resultant surplus of Phantoms proved beneficial to the Air National Guard and Air Force Reserve which began receiving F-4Cs during this period. (Don Spering)

41. F-4C Phantoms continued to be sent to Air National Guard squadrons until as late as 1980, when the 136th Fighter Interceptor Squadron retired its F-101B Voodoos. Fighter Interceptor Squadrons were not part of TAC until 1979, when the Aerospace Defense Command became part of TAC, to form ADTAC. The distinctive grey camouflage applied to ADTAC Phantoms is in marked contrast to the brown/green disruptive scheme applied to TAC Phantoms, and the 'rainbow' rudders on these Niagara Falls-based aircraft emphasize that contrast. (Don Linn)

41▼

▲42

42. The F-101 Voodoo never really served in TAC, having been assigned to Fighter Interceptor Squadrons of Aerospace Defense Command before the latter was absorbed into TAC. During this period three ANG Fighter Interceptor Squadrons were still equipped with the F-101, and one of these, the 111th FIS of the Texas ANG, began to re-equip with F-4Cs during July 1982. (Don Spering)

43. During the late 1970s and early 1980s the Air National Guard and Air Force Reserve were the recipients of many of the Air Force's fleet of F-4Cs, and although these Phantoms were twenty years old (a few were even older) they still proved to be a valuable asset. Pictured are three F-4Cs of the 182nd Tactical Fighter Squadron during a July 1982 training flight. (Don Spering)

44. A Republic F-84F Thunderstreak serving with Tactical Air Command in the mid-1960s. The F-84F was one of TAC's main fighter assets during the previous decade but was superseded by the North American F-100 Super Sabre as TAC's primary fighter-bomber, although it continued to serve in Air Guard and Air Force Reserve squadrons into the early 1970s. This Thunderstreak is serving as a target tug, as evidenced by the target dart under its wing. (Don Linn Collection)

45. A flight-line of North American F-100D Super Sabres of the 166th Tactical Fighter Squadron, photographed in 1975. The prototype YF-100 was first revealed on 25 May 1953, but did not make its first flight until the following year. The Super Sabre served in Vietnam until replaced by the F-4 Phantom and relegated to Air National Guard and Air Force Reserve squadrons, finally to be retired from active service during the late 1970s. (Dick Starinchak)

▼43

44▲ 45▼

▲46

46. A McDonnell Douglas RF-101C photo-reconnaissance Voodoo of the Mississippi Air National Guard, its ground crew completing final pre-flight checks, 1978. On 27 November 1957 an RF-101C flown by Lt. Gus Klatt attained a speed of 781.74mph flying from Los Angeles to New York during 'Operation Sun Run' – a record-breaking trans-America flight. (Don Linn)

47. A pair of LTV A-7D Corsairs of the 112th Tactical Fighter Group on their way to the gunnery range in 1982. The A-7D was first delivered to TAC squadrons in 1968, but by 1978 many were being replaced by A-10s and F-16s and most were transferred to the Air Guard, where the type will continue to serve until the 1990s. (Don Linn)

48. An RF-4C of the Kentucky Air Guard casts its reflection on the rain-soaked ramp at NAS Fallon during 'Photo Derby 82', a photo-reconnaissance competition held every other year. Seven Air National Guard squadrons are equipped with the RF-4C Phantom, augmenting Tactical Air Command's photo-recce force. (Don Linn)

49. An F-4D Phantom of the 89th Tactical Fighter Squadron armed with six Mk 82 500lb bombs and a GAU-5/A gun pod mounted on the centreline during a June 1985 training flight. In Vietnam F-4 Phantoms demonstrated their ability to perform close air support, interdiction and air superiority missions with equal success. (Doug Tachauer)

▼47

48▲ 49▼

▲50

50. The McDonnell Douglas F-4G Wild Weasel is a derivative of the F-4E Phantom equipped with special electronic countermeasures for surface-to-air missile (SAM) suppression. The F-4E and F-4G are the last versions of the Phantom to be purchased by the USAF and TAC, with which Phantoms have served since 1962, beginning with the F-4C. The F-4G pictured here is from the 37th Tactical Fighter Wing. (P. Huston)

▼51

51. A dramatic photograph of an F-4D of the 108th TFW, with blue BD-33 practice bombs on Multiple Ejector Racks (MER) and a GAU-5/A gun pod on the centreline. Since F-4 Phantoms first became operational in the Air National Guard in February 1971, 28 squadrons have been equipped with the four basic types, RF-4C, F-4C, F-4D and F-4E – a total of 700 aircraft in all. (Don Spering)

52▲

52. The red star on the intake splitter plate of this F-4C of the 159th Tactical Fighter Group is a MiG kill carried over from this particular Phantom's Vietnam service. The F-4C was the Air Force's first Phantom, and closely related to the US Navy's F-4B. (Don Spering)

53. Part of TAC training, for both Reserve forces and the regular Air Force, is the interception of aircraft violating US airspace (for example, a Soviet aircraft flying home from Cuba). To help prepare for such tasks B-52 bombers often act out the role of intruders to give TAC fighter squadrons realistic 'targets'. The three F-4Cs seen here are from the 184th Tactical Fighter Squadron, 1981. (Don Spering)

53▼

▲54 ▼55

56▲

54. The 178th Fighter Interceptor Squadron of the North Dakota Air National Guard often flies in cold, snowy conditions in the north-west United States. The 178th FIS ('Happy Hooligans') used to operate F-101s, which were a familiar sight at 'William Tell' competitions, but it is now equipped with F-4D Phantoms. Here a 'Happy Hooligans' Phantom, armed with AIM-9 Sidewinder missiles, taxis out for a competition sortie during the 1984 'William Tell' meet at Tyndall AFB. (Don Spering)

55. An unusual bomb mix is released from a 108th Tactical Fighter Wing F-4D during a low-level pass over the Warren Grove Gunnery and Bombing Range, 15 March 1985 – two Mk 82 500lb bombs, one Snakeye high-drag bomb and a Bullute BSU-49/B AIR (Air Inflatable Retarder) bomb. The F-4D can carry, depending on the type of mission, over 8,000lb of bombs (eleven Mk 117 750lb general purpose bombs) and four missiles. (Don Spering)

56. The crew of an F-4C of the Air Defense Weapons Center at Tyndall AFB prepare for a 1978 training sortie. Air Force Phantom crews are all pilots, unlike the US Navy and Marine Corps crews, whose back-seat RIOs are not (USAF Phantoms have full flight controls in the back seat, whereas Navy F-4s do not). Whether a US Navy or Air Force crew, however, the job of the 'back-seater' is to operate the weapons systems and radars and to provide an extra set of eyes during combat, allowing the pilot in front to concentrate on flying the aircraft. (Don Spering)

57. Crewmen dismount from their 347th Tactical Fighter Wing F-4E (based at Moody AFB, Georgia) at Andrews AFB for the 1984 airshow. This very clean Phantom has recently had 'European I' camouflage applied to both upper and lower surfaces, with subdued national insignia. On the tail is the colourful Tactical Air Command badge, and on the fuselage, just aft of the intakes, is the 347th Wing badge. (Don Linn)

57▼

RESCUE
E11

58. Pilots of New Jersey's 108th Tactical Fighter Wing inspect a batch of Mk 82 bombs during a 'surge' mission in October 1983. Following its return from the sortie, this Phantom was refuelled, given another bomb load and airborne again within thirty minutes. This 'surge' exercise is designed to place the maximum workload on pilots and ground crews. (Don Spering)

▲59

59. 'Wheels in the well' as an F-4E of the 4th Tactical Fighter Wing at Seymour-Johnson AFB takes off for a training mission. The F-4E Phantom completed its first flight on 30 June 1967 and entered operational squadron service the following January with the 33rd Tactical Fighter Wing at Eglin AFB. During November 1968 F-4Es were sent to Vietnam for combat evaluation, and the first European deployment of the F-4E took place during July 1969. (Don Spering)

60. The F-4G Wild Weasel – this example serves with the 35th Tactical Fighter Wing at George AFB – is a further development of the F-4E. The noticeable external differences for the F-4G are the chin pod in place of the Vulcan cannon, and the pod built into the top of the vertical tail. There are a total of 52 new antennas fitted for the APR-38 radar homing and warning system, developed by McDonnell Douglas. The rear cockpit of the F-4G is quite different from that of any other F-4; the instrument panel extends to the top of the canopy, effectively blocking any forward vision. (Don Spering)

61. The classic lines of the Phantom are illustrated here by an RF-4C of the 165th Tactical Reconnaissance Squadron of the Kentucky Air National Guard. The introduction of the RF-4C dramatically changed aerial reconnaissance: in addition to both high- and low-altitude photographic equipment, the aircraft also has infra-red, laser and radar reconnaissance systems. The IR system can detect hidden vehicles and other equipment by their heat signatures. (Don Spering)

62. A trio of RF-4C Phantoms of the 106th Tactical Reconnaissance Squadron on a low-level photo-recce mission. As its designation indicates, the RF-4C is a derivative of the F-4C. On 29 May 1962 SOR (Specific Operational Requirement) 196 was issued for the new variant, and six F-4Bs were purchased from the Navy and reworked on the McDonnell Douglas assembly line to RF-4C test and evaluation aircraft; the first of these made its maiden flight on 8 August 1963. (Don Spering)

▼60

▼61 62▶

▲ 63 ▼ 64

63. In January 1979 TAC's 388th Tactical Fighter Wing at Hill AFB became the first operational F-16 squadron, replacing its F-4 Phantoms. The F-16 was developed to replace the F-4 in the active Air Force and to modernize the reserve forces, and by 1984 there were 750 F-16s serving in USAF fighter squadrons. This F-16A is armed with wingtip-mounted AIM-9 Sidewinder missiles and two Mk 84 2,000lb bombs attached to the underwing pylons. (Don Spering)

64. Two F-16A Falcons of the 428th Tactical Fighter Squadron land at Nellis AFB, April 1983. These Falcons are each fitted with SUU-20 rocket dispensers and 370-gallon fuel tanks. Of interest in this photograph is the concentration evident in the pilot flying the wing position, his head turned to his flight leader, holding position on final approach and maintaining formation integrity. (Doug Tachauer)

65. A flight of four F-16As of the 169th Tactical Fighter Group of the South Carolina ANG during a 1983 training flight from McEntire ANGB. The 169th TFG was the first Air Guard squadron to receive F-16s, trading in its A-7D Corsairs in June 1983. Other Air Guard squadrons are expected to begin conversion to F-16s during 1986; Florida, New Jersey, Montana and Massachusetts Air Guard units are among those scheduled to receive F-16s by 1988. Many of these squadrons are now flying F-106 Delta Darts, which in turn will be retired from service, perhaps to become drones. (Don Linn)

65▼

▲66

66. The Air Force Reserve began receiving F-16s during October 1983. The 419th Tactical Fighter Wing at Hill AFB was selected as the first Air Force Reserve F-16 squadron, replacing the unit's F-105D Thunderchiefs. The proficiency of the 419th's members in flying and maintaining the F-16 during their first full year of operations earned the unit the Tactical Air Command's Flying Safety Award. (Don Linn)

67. A MacDill AFB-based F-16A of the 61st Tactical Fighter Training Squadron arrives at London, Ontario, for the 1985 air show. The container on the port wing's outer pylon is for carrying the pilot's personal belongings on extended deployments and cross-country flights. On the centreline is a 370-gallon fuel tank. (Don Spering)

68. A force equal to that of eight locomotives powers each of these 405th Tactical Training Wing F-15 Eagles climbing above the Arizona desert near Luke AFB. The largest fighter pilot training base in the free world, Luke AFB trains both F-15 and F-16 aircrews, and also conducts F-5 training for foreign fighter pilots. The facility was named in honour of Lt Frank Luke, the 'balloon-busting' ace of the First World War killed in France in 1918. (McDonnell Douglas)

69. An F-15 Eagle of the 318th Fighter Interceptor Squadron fires an AIM-7 Sparrow missile at a target drone during a recent exercise. The 318th FIS made its transition from the F-106 to the F-15 in 1984. The F-15 has served with Tactical Air Command since the 1970s, progressively replacing the F-4 Phantom as the USAF's primary air superiority fighter. The original F-15A and the two-seat F-15B were followed in June 1979 by the F-15C and two-seat F-15D. (McDonnell Douglas)

▼67

68▲ 69▼

▲70

70. In January 1982 the 48th Fighter Interceptor Squadron at Langley AFB re-equipped with F-15A Eagles, thereby ending more than twenty years of F-106 service. Illustrated here is one of the squadron's first F-15As over the partially frozen James River. The squadron's distinctive blue and white rudder stripes and tail chevron are similar to the markings carried on the 48th's F-106s. (Don Linn)
71. The 1st Tactical Fighter Wing, based at Langley AFB (which is also the headquarters of Tactical Air Command), comprises three F-15 units, the 27th, 71st and 94th Fighter Squadrons. This new F-15C, loaded with eighteen Mk 82 500lb bombs, is fitted with conformal fuel tanks; located along the fuselage aft of the intakes, the CFTs considerably increase fuel capacity with no significant drag penalty. The F-15C also has an internal fuel capacity 2,000lb greater than that of earlier marks. (Don Spering)
72. During September 1985 this F-15C participated in tests for the USAF's new Low Altitude Navigation and Targeting Infrared for Night (LANTIRN) system; the pod for this equipment is located under the F-15's port intake. These trials marked an important step in the development of the new F-15E, a dual-role fighter which will serve as a fighter-bomber while still retaining the exceptional air superiority capabilities of current F-15s. (McDonnell Douglas)

71▲ 72▼

▲73

73. The two-tone grey scheme on this A-10 was first thought to be an effective camouflage against enemy fighters, but the opposite is actually true. The A-10 was designed as a tank killer, but radars have steadily become more sophisticated and accurate, forcing the A-10 to fly close to the ground to evade enemy radars. At low level the two-tone grey scheme stood out over a forest of green, or a brown desert, making an easy target for enemy fighters looking down. A new, more practical, camouflage scheme was therefore developed. (Fairchild)

74. The Air National Guard began receiving A-10s in 1981, the first time a front-line aircraft had been assigned to ANG units. At present five Air Guard squadrons are equipped with A-10s, and five Air Force Reserve squadrons. The aircraft can attain a combat speed at sea level of 425mph, can range 288 miles with 9,500lb of ordnance, and can loiter for two hours with a twenty minute reserve. (Don Spering)

75. A close-up view of the A-10's 30mm GAU-8/A multi-barrel 'tank-killing' cannon, showing the new collar added to disperse gases. The A-10's gun is accurate within a range of 5,000ft. (Don Spering)

▼74

75▶

LIAS

▲76

76. This A-10 of the New York Air Guard's 138th Tactical Fighter Squadron ('The Boys from Syracuse') illustrates the effectiveness of the A-10's new camouflage. The engines are mounted high on the fuselage to reduce the possibility of debris ingestion during sorties at very low level. (Don Spering)

77. In 1983 the 176th Tactical Fighter Squadron of the Wisconsin Air National Guard became the last ANG squadron to equip with A-10s, bringing the total number of Air Guard A-10 squadrons to five. Here, the A-10 on the right has its refuelling receptacle door open, waiting its turn at the KC-135 tanker. Each aircraft is fitted with AGM-65 Mavericks with the warheads removed, allowing the missile's TV camera to be used as a combat camera to score gun runs. (Don Spering)

▼77

78▲

78. The new F-16XL shows its distinctive 'cranked-arrow' wing design. The F-16XL and the new F-15E are competing for the USAF's new dual-role fighter requirement. Both aircraft are being called on to perform both air-to-air and deep interdiction roles, by day and night and in adverse weather. The decision as to which of these two fighters will be the successful contender is not expected until 1987, but it is likely that a place will be found for both.

79. A pair of McDonnell Douglas F-15A Eagles of the 1st Tactical Fighter Wing during a 1980 training flight. The black and white stripes applied to the fuselage near the wing root on the lead F-15 are believed to be 'Aggressor' identification marks for inter-squadron air combat training. The F-15 is currently TAC's – and the USAF's – best operational fighter. (Don Linn)

79▼

▲80

80. A test-squadron F-15A fitted with BUU-20 rocket launchers during a 1984 flight. The F-15 is the first US fighter with engines which produce thrust greater than the weight of the loaded aircraft, a virtue achieved by the use of boron-epoxy composite, honeycomb and titanium materials to reduce weight, and of high-technology, high-thrust engines. (K. Svendsen)

81. A full bomb load is carried by this F-111A of the 366th Tactical Fighter Wing from Mountain Home AFB. The F-111 is a twin-engined, two-seat tactical strike aircraft. It can operate at night, at low levels in all weather conditions, and at supersonic speeds to altitudes above 60,000ft. There are only three wings of F-111s in the US Air Force, with 72 aircraft per wing. The new F-15E will augment the F-111 force when it is introduced in 1988. (USAF)

82. The last regular Air Force squadron to operate the F-106 Delta Dart is the 49th Fighter Interceptor Squadron at Griffiss AFB, New York. The 49th FIS will convert to F-15A Eagles by June 1986 and its aircraft will incorporate the same eagle motif as seen on this F-106. Of special interest in this November 1985 photograph is the 20mm gun pod located on the undersides of the F-106, between the landing gear doors. These pods are now a standard item on Delta Darts. (Don Linn)

83. A Northrop F-5E of the 57th Fighter Weapons Wing in one of the many multi-coloured camouflage schemes with which these 'Aggressor' aircraft are associated. The F-5E is the US aircraft best able to simulate Soviet fighter characteristics, and the various colour schemes help to convey the impression of a hostile aircraft in air combat training exercises. (D. F. Brown)

▼81

82▲ 83▼

▲84 ▼85

86▲

84. An EB-57 Canberra of the 158th Defense Systems Evaluation Squadron during a 1981 sortie. The B-57 was derived from the English Electric Canberra and built under licence by the Martin Aircraft Company of Baltimore. During the Vietnam War B-57s flew close-support bombing missions, and the modified B-57G flew night interdiction missions against North Vietnamese targets. In 1982 the 158th retired the Canberra and re-equipped with F-4C Phantoms. (Don Linn)

85. The Air National Guard is TAC's last operator of the Convair C-131 transport. The C-131 was assigned to fighter squadrons as a support aircraft but by 1985 only a few remained in active service and by 1987 most, if not all, of these will have been retired. The C-131 seen here is serving with the 159th Fighter Interceptor Squadron of the Florida Air Guard, and was photographed over Jacksonville on its return from a training flight in 1985. (Don Linn)

86. The pilot of an A-10 from the 'Flying Yankees' of the Connecticut Air Guard goes over his flight check list prior to take-off. A Maverick TV guided missile is located under the port wing. The squadron badge affixed to the engine pod comprises a running Pilgrim. The A-10 first entered operational service in March 1976 with the 355th Tactical Fighter Training Wing at Davis-Monthan AFB, Arizona. (Don Linn)

87. A pair of A-10s from the 138th Tactical Fighter Squadron depart for a training flight. The Thunderbolt II is the first USAF aircraft to be designed specifically for the close air support of surface forces. It has excellent manoeuvrability at low speeds and a highly accurate weapons delivery system. There is a bullet-proof wind-screen, and the pilot is enclosed by titanium armor plate, which also protects the flight control system from hostile fire. (Don Linn)

87▼

▲88

88. The 48th Fighter Interceptor Squadron at Langley AFB converted from F-106 Delta Darts to F-15 Eagles in 1981. Pictured here is the squadron's last F-106 on its final flight during the late morning of 11 January 1982. The arrival of F-15s for the 48th at Langley – as the first Air Defense squadron to equip with the Eagle – marked the end of twenty-one years of F-106 service. (Don Linn)
89. An F-106A of the 5th Fighter Interceptor Squadron 'Spittin' Kittens' lands at Nellis AFB during 'Green Flag 83-1', April 1983. 'Green Flag' exercises focus on co-ordinating and increasing the electronic combat capabilities of tactical air forces, and scenarios are developed to test and evaluate current and proposed electronic combat systems. A combined 'Green Flag' and 'Red Flag' exercise is conducted annually to provide realistic training for aircrews in electronic warfare tactics, and to test the effectiveness of electronic countermeasures. In 1984 the 5th FIS was disbanded and its F-106s dispersed among the remaining F-106 squadrons. (Doug Tachauer)
90. By 1985 the F-106 was nearing the end of its Air Force career, and only one regular USAF squadron remained, along with five Air National Guard squadrons. One of these ANG squadrons was Florida's 159th FIS, aircraft from which are seen here flying over Jacksonville in a photograph which also compares the appearance of the F-106A with that of the two-seat F-106B. Produced in fewer numbers than any of the other 'Century Series' fighters, the F-106 could perhaps be considered the most successful, meeting all the demands requested of it for twenty-seven years! (Don Spering)

89▲ 90▼

▲91

91. A flight of four F-106s from New Jersey's 177th Fighter Interceptor Group at Atlantic City, in diamond formation during a 1981 training mission over the Atlantic. The maiden flight of the F-106 took place during December 1956, but the first F-106 meeting all production requirements took a further two and a half years to enter operational service. (Don Spering)

92. Three F-106s of the 87th Fighter Interceptor Squadron 'Red Bulls', from K.I. Sawyer AFB, on the flight-line at Tyndall AFB during the 1984 'William Tell' meet. The 87th FIS has since been disbanded and its aircraft dispersed among the remaining F-106 squadrons. (Don Spering)

93. The flight-line of the Massachusetts Air Guard's 101st Fighter Interceptor Squadron ('Seagulls') at Otis AFB, Cape Cod. These Delta Darts have the later 'blown bubble' canopy, a modification introduced during the mid-1970s to replace the original production fit that incorporated a frame that ran lengthwise through the top, effectively restricting the pilot's view. (Don Spering)

94. The five remaining National Guard squadrons usingF-106s will begin the transition to F-16s in 1986, bringing F-106 operational service to a complete end by 1988–89 after thirty-four years – a record for a fighter aircraft. Pictured here are four 49th FIS Delta darts refuelling from a 41st Air Refueling Squadron KC-135 tanker during a November 1985 training flight. (Don Linn)

▼92

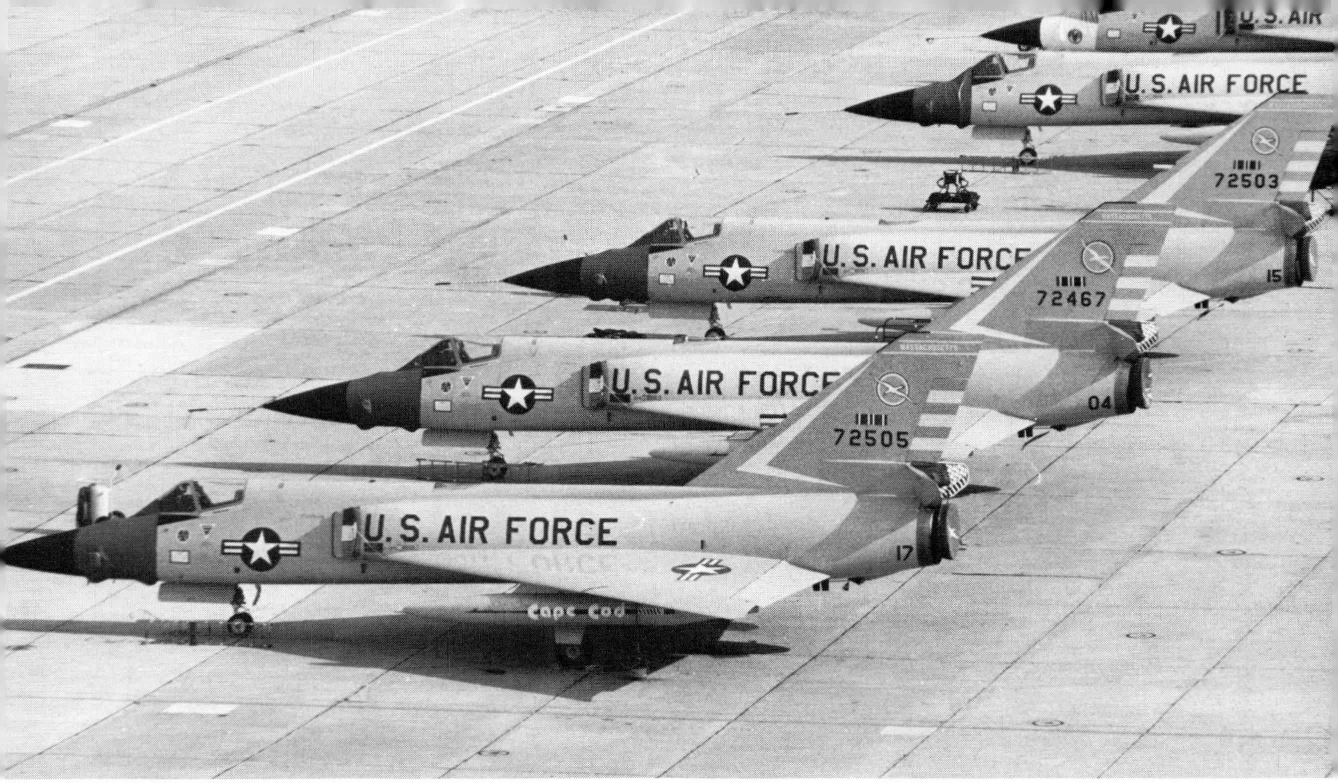

U.S. AIR FORCE
72503
U.S. AIR FORCE
72467
15
U.S. AIR FORCE
72505
04
U.S. AIR FORCE
17
Cape Cod

93▲ 94▼

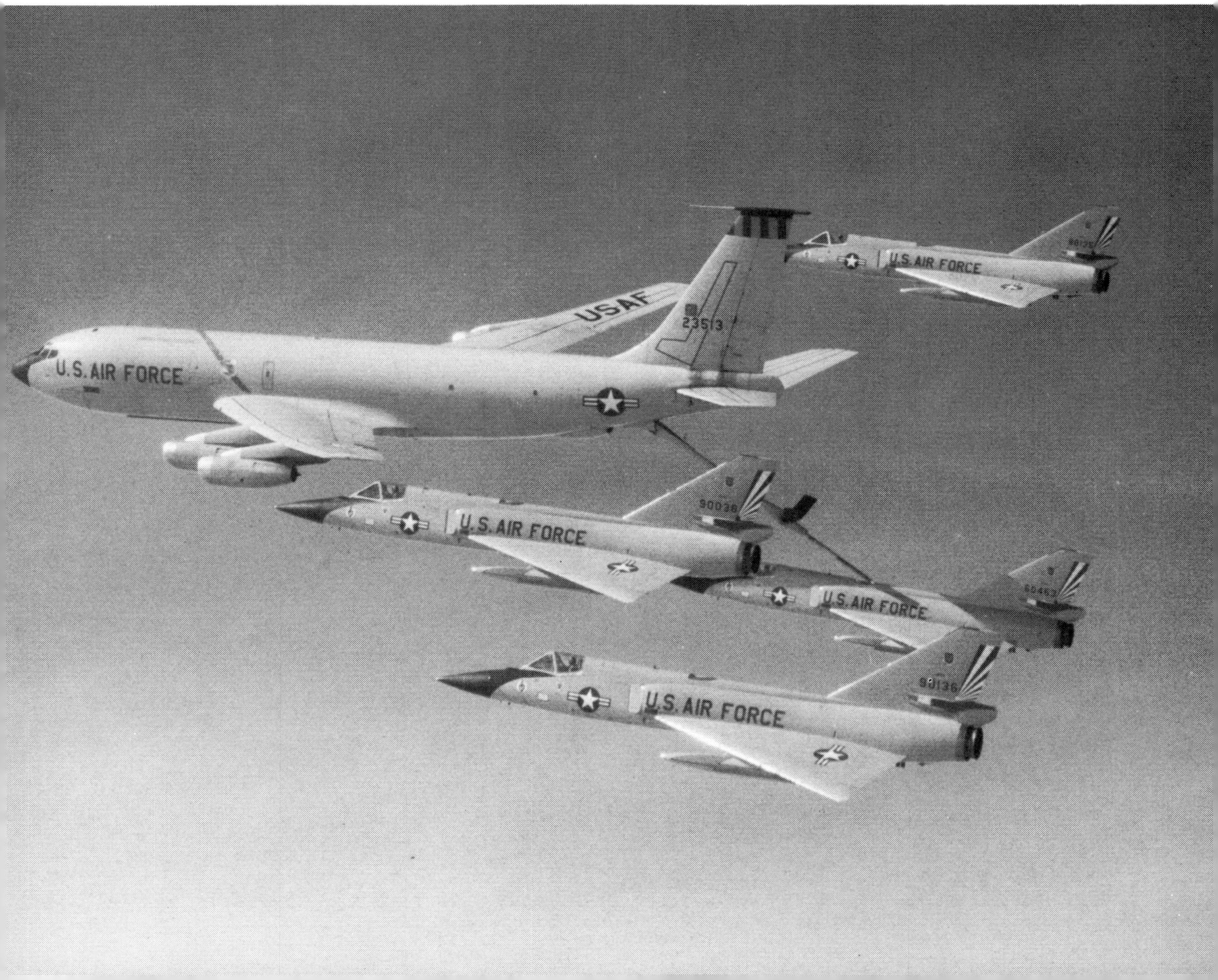

USAF
23513
U.S. AIR FORCE
U.S. AIR FORCE
90036
U.S. AIR FORCE
U.S. AIR FORCE
90136
U.S. AIR FORCE

▲95

95. The F-111 represents the USAF's, and Tactical Air Command's, only current long-range, 'around-the-clock' interdiction fighter. Four versions of this variable-geometry aircraft are currently in service with the USAF. Deliveries began in October 1967 and a total of 141 production F-111As were built, serving with distinction during the Vietnam War. The 366th Tactical Fighter Wing is now the only Tactical Air Command squadron operating the -A variant; an example is pictured here. (USAF)

96. An F-111D of the 27th Tactical Fighter Wing at Cannon AFB (easily identified by the 'CC' tail codes), showing to advantage the aircraft's clean lines. The F-111D was designed with advanced avionics, offering improvements in navigation and air-to-air weapons delivery. Ninety-seven examples were produced by General Dynamics. (Don Spering)

97. F-111s are always popular at air shows: here one is directed to the parking ramp for participation in the 1985 London International Airshow at Ontario, Canada, which paid tribute to the F-111's twentieth anniversary. Air crews gain access to the F-111's cockpit by climbing up the side of the fuselage using built-in hand holds, or crew ladders, and enter through the canopy sides, which swing upwards as illustrated here. (Don Spering)

▼96

97▶

London
International
Air Show

▲98

▲99 ▼100

98. The USAF's *Thunderbirds* aerial demonstration team is one of Tactical Air Command's most famous, and visible, squadrons, and has alway flown aircraft currently assigned to TAC. The T-38 was first introduced to the team in 1973, after four seasons flying the F-4 Phantom, the decision to switch being concerned primarily with the high cost of fuel. The T-38s were replaced by F-16s in 1983. (USAF)

99. An F-5E 'Aggressor' of the 57th Fighter Weapons Wing lands at Nellis AFB, March 1983. The F-5Es and T-38s assigned to the 57th FWW are painted in various multi-colour camouflage schemes to help simulate air combat training with dissimilar aircraft. The Tactical Fighter Weapons Center at Nellis is responsible for advanced fighter weapons training for mission-ready air crews throughout the USAF. (Doug Tachauer)

100. A 1976 photograph of a T-38 assigned to the 49th Tactical Fighter Wing at Holloman AFB as a support aircraft. T-38s are usually associated with the Training Command, but several have been assigned to fighter units. The T-38 was derived from Northrop's F-5A 'Freedom Fighter', and was in continuous production from 1956 to 1972. A total of 1,187 were produced by Northrop, more than 1,100 of these being delivered to the USAF. (Don Spering)

101. The 479th Tactical Training Wing is equipped with AT-38Bs for its job of teaching novice fighter pilots the basics of their craft. The 479th TTW's four flying squadrons are equipped with 131 two-seat AT-38B Talons and 160 instructors to teach 'lead-in' fighter training to pilots just out of undergraduate pilot and navigation school and scheduled for fighter assignments. The 479th TTW is the only USAF squadron equipped with the AT-38B, five of which (it has been reported) can be operated for the cost of one F-15. (Don Linn)
102. An EB-57 Canberra of the 158th Defense Systems Evaluation Group, Vermont Air National Guard, on a 1980 electronic counter-measures training sortie near the New York-Canadian border. The Vermont Air Guard was the last operational B-57 squadron in the USAF, and by the end of 1980 the 158th DSEG began converting to F-4C Phantoms. B-57s served in Vietnam as close air support bombers, and the B-57G version flew night interdiction missions against the infamous Ho Chi Minh trail for two years, 1970–72. (Don Linn)
103. A head-on view of a black B-57C of the 158th Defense Systems Evaluation Squadron during a low-level flight demonstration. This particular version of the Martin-built Canberra ended its career with the Vermont Air Guard as a training aircraft, utilizing its dual cockpit controls for instructor-student check rides. Only two examples of the B-57C survived by 1980, both painted black with either red or white lettering. (Geoff LeBaron)

101▲

102▲ 103▼

▲104

105 

◀106

104. The latest version of the F-111 serving with Tactical Air Command is the EF-111A Raven, an electronic countermeasures variant. The EF-111A is a conversion of the F-111A airframe, completed by Grumman and fitted with mainly off-the-shelf components that enable it to accomplish defense suppression measures. Fifty-two EF-111As are being produced for missions that include barrier surveillance jamming, suppression of SAM threats during close air support operations, and jamming for deep strike missions. The first EF-111s were delivered to the 366th Tactical Fighter Wing in late 1981. (Don Linn)

105. The T-33 is the oldest aircraft still actively serving in TAC, and the oldest T-33 (serial 52-734) could be found serving with the 48th FIS in 1984. This particular T-33 was, as its serial number indicates, built in 1952, and when TAC celebrates its fortieth anniversary in 1986 this aircraft, if still flying, will be 34 years old – almost the same age as Tactical Air Command itself! (Don Linn)

106. Several T-33s still equip the Air National Guard, carrying out a variety of duties. This T-33 of the Texas Air National Guard's 111th Fighter Interceptor Squadron, based at Ellington AFB in 1982, is acting as an airborne interception target for F-4C fighters. T-33s acting in this role are sometimes equipped with ECM sensors and chaff dispensers to provide added realism. (Don Spering)

▲107 ▼108

109▲

107. An OV-10A of the 601st Tactical Control Wing. The OV-10 was designed by North American for the FAC mission and as a limited quick-response ground support aircraft. A total of 157 were purchased for the USAF, from a production run that lasted only from 1967 to 1969. Powered by two Garrett T-76 turboprops of 715hp each, the aircraft has a maximum speed at sea level of 281mph and a service ceiling of 28,000ft. (Don Spering)

108. Even the OV-10 cannot escape the new 'European I' tactical camouflage, as illustrated by this Bronco of the 1st Special Operations Wing. Broncos are armed with four fixed M60 machine guns mounted in fuselage sponsons. Four sponson hardpoints permit a load of up to 2,400lb, and a centreline hardpoint can carry 1,200lb. (Don Spering)

109. An O-2A of the 507th Tactical Air Control Wing at Shaw AFB photographed during May 1985. A total of 346 specially equipped variants of Cessna's 337 Skymaster entered USAF service in 1966, originally to replace the Cessna O-1 Bird Dog in the FAC role in Vietnam. Although A-37s and OV-10s have replaced many of the O-2s, a few still remained in active TAC and Air Guard service in1985. (Don Spering)

110. A Pennsylvania Air Guard O-2A on a 1982 FAC training mission with rocket launchers attached under the wing. During Vietnam the O-2 FACs would use their rockets to mark enemy targets for the faster moving jet fighter-bombers to attack but could do no real damage themselves. (Don Linn)

110▼

▲111 ▼112

111. An O-2A of the 137th Tactical Air Support Squadron passes over a railway bridge on its way to the target area in 1970. FAC aircraft were painted in this overall grey scheme so that they would stand out over the green jungle and thus be more visible to the higher flying fighters and bombers. The O-2s were unarmed except for their smoke rockets, but the pilots would often take along a few hand grenades for their satisfaction. (Don Spering)

112. A Cessna O-1E Bird Dog in Vietnam in the early 1970s. The O-1 was developed for the US Army as a light liaison and reconnaissance aircraft in 1950. A total of 3,431 were produced – a respectable number – and the USAF selected the aircraft for Forward Air Controller duties in Vietnam owing to its ability to fly 'low and slow', thus allowing the pilot a better opportunity to spot enemy troop and vehicle movements. O-1 and O-2 FACs were generally referred to as 'unarmed and unafraid', and highly respected for the job they did in Vietnam. (Don Spering)

113. An O-1F serving with the 21st Tactical Air Support Group at Phu Cat Air Base, Vietnam, in 1970. The O-1 served gallantly until replaced by the twin-engined, 'push-pull' Cessna O-2 and the first Cessna jet, the A-37. O-1s saw service in Air National Guard and Air Force Reserve squadrons during the 1970s, but by 1980 all had been retired from active service. (Taylor/Spering)

114. Fixed-wing types are not the only aircraft serving with Tactical Air Command: helicopters, too, are operated in significant numbers. Several varieties equip TAC, including Sikorsky's HH-53 and H-3 and several variants of the Bell UH-1 Huey. Pictured here is a UH-1P assigned to the 1st Tactical Fighter Wing at Langley AFB. The UH-1P was first ordered for duty in Vietnam for classified psychological warfare missions, but most Hueys assigned to TAC bases now perform local rescue duties. (Don Spering)

113▲ 114▼

▲115 ▼116

117▲

115. The first Tactical Air Command unit to receive Boeing's E-3A AWACS was the 552nd AEW&C Group in 1977. The E-3A, based on the Boeing 707-320B airframe, carries a 30ft rotating radar dish. It is capable of controlling any aspect of the air effort, including air superiority, strike, support, interdiction and airlift, and its radar is able to detect and track low-flying aircraft by eliminating ground clutter. (USAF)

116. Initially the USAF ordered 34 Boeing E-3A AWACS, with deliveries beginning in 1977, and an additional 18 E-3s were ordered by NATO to upgrade the communications for and control of its air defence forces. Each of the first 24 E-3As is now being updated to E-3B standards. Improvements include faster computer capabilities, anti-jam communications, an austere maritime surveillance capability, additional radio communications, and five extra display consoles. The first E-3B was delivered to the 522nd AWACW in July 1984. (Don Spering)

117. The EC-135K is a KC-135 modified for special missions. Thirty-nine tankers were converted for airborne command and control, including the control of Tactical Air Command fighters during overseas deployments. EC-135 aircraft currently serve with TAC, and also SAC, PACAF and USAFE. They are fitted with extensive communications equipment. Pictured here is the first EC-135K (modified from the first KC-135A), serving with the 8th Tactical Deployment Control Squadron in 1977. (Don Spering)

▲118

118. A C-47D of the 1st Special Operations Wing in 1972. The venerable 'Gooney Bird' has certainly paid for itself many times over since first entering US Army Air Corps service in the early 1940s. During the Vietnam War the C-47 performed in many roles, including that of a gunship, but by the end of the 1980s none remained on the USAF inventory. (Don Spering)

119. A EC-121S of the 193rd Tactical Electronics Warfare Squadron of the Pennsylvania Air Guard at Harrisburg in 1973. Of special interest is the absence of any identifying markings, including national insignia. During Vietnam EC-121s flew nearly 14,000 combat sorties between 1965 and 1974. These AWAC 'Connies' helped to vector fighters to MiG threats and assisted in the recovery of stranded air crew. By the mid-1970s EC-121s were being replaced by EC-135s. (Don Spering)

▼119

120▲

120. Convair C-131s have served with Tactical Air Command since 1952. This C-131D displays the typical paint scheme of the early 1960s – a silver and white fuselage with 'day-glo' nose, tail and wingtips, and a TAC badge on its tail. The aircraft's unit is unknown, but a three-star general's placard appears aft of the cockpit windscreen. (Don Spering)

121. Similar in configuration to the C-131, this CT-29 of the Illinois Air Guard's 170th Tactical Fighter Squadron wears the Vietnam-era camouflage applied to all tactical aircraft during, and after, the war. Both the C-131 and CT-29, which performed as support aircraft in tactical fighter squadrons, are based on the CV-240 Convair-liner, and a total of 272 were purchased by the USAF. (Don Spering)

121▼

▲122 ▼123

124▲

122. Fairchild C-123K transports also served with TAC, as illustrated by this aircraft of the 302nd Tactical Airlift Wing. C-123s and C-130s were important assets to TAC and served until 1974, when all tactical airlift forces were transferred to the Military Airlift Command (MAC). The twin-engined C-123s were noisy and uncomfortable, but they performed vital medium transport duties. (Don Spering)
123. A C-118 Liftmaster serving with TAC in 1973 sits on the ramp at McGuire AFB awaiting its crew for another flight. Liftmasters entered TAC service in the late 1950s but were transferred to MAC in 1974 along with all the other transport assets of TAC. The Douglas built C-118 is the military version of the DC-6 passenger airliner and last served with the US Navy in 1984. (Don Spering)
124. Several De Havilland C-7 Caribous served with TAC; this one is from the 150th Tactical Airlift Squadron of the New Jersey Air Guard, 1973. The C-7A was first transferred from the US Army in 1967, and provided TAC with an excellent light transport with STOL capabilities. (Don Spering)
125. An AC-119K gunship of the 1st Special Operations Wing in Vietnam during 1970. This was the third gunship series, its predecessors being the AC-47 and the AC-130, and it was produced to allow C-130s to be retained for transport duties. (Don Spering)

125▼

▲126 ▼127

126. A DC-130A of the 11th Tactical Drone Squadron, 355th Tactical Fighter Wing, Davis-Monthan AFB, 1973. These drone controller DC-130s may be readily identified by the longer radome nose with its additional pod, and by the large underwing pylons for drone attachment. The DC-130 is capable of carrying four Firebee RPVs (remotely piloted vehicles). (Don Spering)
127. The original C-130As were first produced without the nose radomes common to later C-130s and were often referred to as 'Roman Nose' C-130s. This example was serving with the 327th Tactical Airlift Squadron of the Air Force Reserve in 1972. Almost a dozen remain in active MAC service with Air National Guard and Air Force Reserve squadrons. (Don Spering)
128. Another gunship version is the black AC-130 of the 1st Special Operations Wing. These Air Force Reserve aircraft, transferred to MAC in 1974 and referred to as 'Spectres', were, with their assortment of machine guns, cannon, and twin 40mm Bofors guns, the most heavily armed aircraft in Vietnam. Little was left standing when one of the Spectre gunships opened fire on a ground target. (Don Spering)

128▲

▲129

129. Although most C-130s had been transferred to MAC in 1974, a few, like this EC-130, are still assigned to Tactical Air Command. The large blade antenna that runs from the vertical tail to the fuselage spine is the identifying feature for this EC-130, but other less conspicuous antennas are also fitted to the fuselage sides and under the wings. The actual mission of this special electronic Hercules is classified, but it is generally known to have some type of communications jamming function. This machine belongs to the 193rd Special Operations Group of the Pennsylvania Air National Guard. (Don Linn)

130. An early-model C-130B Hercules in natural metal finish, photographed in 1963 when participating in 'Swift Strike III', a joint US Army and USAF exercise. Developed more than thirty years ago, the C-130 Hercules remains in production, with basic and specialized versions continuing to perform many different roles worldwide. (Don Spering)

▼130